THE G. SCHIRMER VIOLA ANTHOLOGY

11 WORKS FROM THE 20TH AND 21ST CENTURIES

ISBN 978-1-4803-9526-8

ED 4572

G. SCHIRMER, Inc.

DISTRIBUTED BY

7777 W. BLUEMOUND RD. P.O. BOX 13819 MILWAUKEE, WI 53213

www.musicsalesclassical.com
www.halleonard.com

CONTENTS

Music appears in the viola part only.

NOTES ON THE MUSIC

Ernest Bloch (1880–1959)
LENTO
third movement from Suite for Viola and Piano

Date of Composition: May 1919. Dedication: "To Mrs. F. S. Coolidge." First Performance: 27 September 1919, Pittsfield, Massachusetts, Louis Bailly, viola, Harold Bauer, piano. First Publication: G. Schirmer, Inc., 1920.

In a departure from the Jewish-themed works for which Bloch had become known in the 1910s, the Suite for Viola and Piano is colored by Far Eastern influences and originally featured programmatic titles. The third movement was inspired by a friend's account of nocturnal travels through Javanese villages and the sounds of wooden musical instruments he heard there. The suite won the Coolidge Prize in 1919 in a competition at the Berkshire Festival of Chamber Music sponsored by Elizabeth Sprague Coolidge, a prolific patron of chamber music in the United States in the early twentieth century to whom the work is dedicated. Rebecca Clarke's viola sonata originally tied with Bloch's piece for first place, but Coolidge cast her vote for Bloch when asked to break the tie. Both works went on to become staples of the viola repertory.

MEDITATION AND PROCESSIONAL

Date of Composition: 1951. Dedication: "Dedicated to Milton Preves." First Publication: G. Schirmer, Inc., 1954.

A talented violinist as well as a composer, Swiss-born Ernest Bloch studied at the conservatory in Brussels with Eugène Ysaÿe (violin) and François Rasse (composition). In 1916, following further study in Paris and conducting positions in France and Switzerland, Bloch settled in the United States, eventually becoming a U.S. citizen. He was the first composition teacher at the David Mannes College of Music in New York City, and later went on to become the founding musical director for the Cleveland Institute of Music and the director of the San Francisco Conservatory of Music.

Ernest Bloch composed *Meditation and Processional* following a week-long festival celebrating his seventieth birthday in Chicago in December 1950. Violist and Chicago Symphony Orchestra member Milton Preves had performed Bloch's Suite for Viola and Orchestra at the festival so beautifully that Bloch dedicated to him these two brief, melodic movements. Originally written for viola and piano, Bloch later arranged the piece for violin and piano and composed an orchestral version of the accompaniment.

PROCESSIONAL
second movement from
Suite hébraïque for Viola and Piano

Date of Composition: 1951. Dedication: "To the Covenant Club of Illinois." First Performance (orchestral version): 1 January 1953, Chicago, Milton Preves, viola, Chicago Symphony Orchestra, Rafael Kubelik, conductor. First Publication: G. Schirmer, Inc., 1953.

Ernest Bloch composed *Suite hébraïque* along with *Meditation and Processional*, originally conceiving of the piece as one five-movement work. After splitting the composition into two separate pieces, Bloch sent the three movements of *Suite hébraïque*, (I. Rapsodie, II. Processional, III. Affirmation) to Chicago's Covenant Club as a thank you for sponsoring a December 1950 festival honoring his seventieth birthday. *Suite hébraïque* marks a return to the Jewish-themed works for which he had become well known earlier in his career, such as *Schelomo* (1916), a Hebraic rhapsody for cello and orchestra, and the symphony Israel (1916). As in these earlier works, *Suite hébraïque* associates itself with Jewish music through augmented intervals, melismatic melodic lines, and a sense of rhythmic freedom.

Rebecca Clarke (1886–1979)
PASSACAGLIA ON AN OLD ENGLISH TUNE

Date of Composition: 1941. Dedication: "To BB." First Performance: 28 March 1941, Temple Emanu-El, New York City, Rebecca Clarke, viola. First Publication: G. Schirmer, Inc., 1943.

Born in London to a German mother and American father, Clarke moved back and forth between England and the United States throughout her adult life. In her late teens she embarked on an active performing career as a violist. Her most famous compositions are the Viola Sonata (1919) and Piano Trio (1921), both of which combine post-Romantic German sonata form style with aspects of Impressionism. A great deal of her compositional output is owned by her estate and has not yet been published, but increased interest in recent years may cause more works to become available to the public and provide an improved understanding of her significance as a composer.

Clarke wrote the *Passacaglia on an Old English Tune* after returning to the United States from London. This was her second extended residence in the U.S., necessitated by the outbreak of World War II. BB, to whom the work was dedicated, was a nickname for Clarke's niece Magdalen. However, other B's on Clarke's mind at the time may have factored into the dedication. A longing for Britain, exemplified in the use of a theme by Thomas Tallis, was likely intensified by the death of Frank Bridge on 10 January 1941. Clarke had also recently been in touch with Bridge's pupil Benjamin Britten regarding her participation in a memorial concert he was organizing for his deceased mentor. Liane Curtis writes that the Passacaglia "can be seen as Clarke's meditation on things British, her friends and colleagues, and the musical life of London, the city she considered her home."[1]

[1]Liane Curtis, "Rebecca Clarke and the British Musical Renaissance," in *A Rebecca Clarke Reader* (Bloomington, IN: Indiana University Press, 2004), 36-37.

John Corigliano (b. 1938)
FANCY ON A BACH AIR

Date of Composition: 1996. First Performance: 24 August 1997, Jordan Hall, Boston, Yo-Yo Ma, cello. First Publication: G. Schirmer, Inc., August 2006. Duration: 6½ minutes.

John Corigliano's music is noted for its combination of the traditional with the avant-garde. He received the Grawemeyer Award for his Symphony No. 1 (1991), and the Pulitzer Prize for his Symphony No. 2 (2001). In addition to the concert hall, Corigliano's music has appeared on stage and screen. His opera The Ghosts of Versailles (1991) has enjoyed several productions and his film score to The Red Violin, recorded by Joshua Bell, won an Academy Award in 1999. Corigliano serves on the composition faculty at the Juilliard School and is Distinguished Professor of Music at Lehman College, City University of New York.

Composer's note from the original publication:

This piece began in celebration and ended in memoriam. My cousin introduced me to his colleague Robert Goldberg and his wife Judy, avid music lovers both. We became fast friends. When later they asked me to compose a piece for their 25th wedding anniversary, I suggested, that instead of a single writer, they ask a group of composers to write variations. And what better theme to choose than the venerable melody of the variations that bore their name? Bach would surely approve.

Their close friends Yo-Yo Ma and Emanuel Ax agreed to play the variations. Then tragedy struck. Robert succumbed to a virulent cancer and died all too soon.

Judy's spirit and love led her to transform what might have been a requiem into a celebration of her husband's life, and Ma and Ax performed the set of Variations preceded by the Bach theme in Boston where the Goldbergs live.

My "Goldberg Variation," Fancy on a Bach Air, is for unaccompanied cello. It transforms the gentle arches of Bach's theme into slowly soaring arpeggi of almost unending phrase-lengths. Its dual inspiration was the love of two extraordinary people and the solo cello suites of a great composer – both of them strong, long-lined, passionate, eternal, and for me, definitive of all that is beautiful in life.

—John Corigliano

John Harbison (b. 1938)
THE VIOLIST'S NOTEBOOK, BOOK ONE
I. Marcus Thompson
II. Betty Hauck
III. James Dunham
IV. Kim Kashkashian
V. Mary Ruth Ray
VI. Marcus Thompson

Date of Composition: 2000. First Publication: Associated Music Publishers, Inc., 2006.

American composer John Harbison was heavily influenced by jazz as a child, performing as the pianist of his own jazz band by age eleven. Two other major influences include Bach and Stravinsky, in particular Bach's cantatas. His works often combine jazz harmony with neo-classical and serialist elements. Harbison received his BA from Harvard University where he studied with Walter Piston. He also studied with Boris Blacher at the Berlin Musikhochschule, as well as with Roger Sessions and Earl Kim at Princeton. In 1987 he was awarded a Pulitzer Prize for *The Flight into Egypt* and in 1989 he was granted a MacArthur Fellowship. Harbison became a professor at the Massachusetts Institute of Technology in 1969 and has been an MIT Honorary Institute Professor since 1996.

Composer's note from the original publication:

The name Bartolomeo Campanioli is lost in the mists of history. I confess that I know nothing about him except that he wrote viola etudes – inventive, musical, satisfying viola etudes. In general no pedagogical etudes need have any place in the education of a musician (I remember especially the miserable pedantry of the famous Kreutzer violin studies). But Campanioli is recalled by a few violists as a good composer (probably a violist himself), a congenial spirit, a musician who encouraged us to expand our technique by dangling an elegantly musical carrot on a stick.

As I began keeping my violist's notebooks I thought of Campanioli, his practical, subversively challenging communications with his violist colleagues. Book I was accumulated, in the margins of larger pieces, over three years. Book II was composed in six days, one a day, as a self-imposed project, at Bogliasco, near Genoa.

These etudes are more compositional than technical studies. Each is dedicated to a violist, mostly hard-core but a few doublers are included. The pieces can be performed in any sequence or grouping.

—John Harbison
January 2003

Karel Husa (b. 1921)
ELEGIE
second movement from Suite for Viola and Piano, Op. 5

Date of Composition: 1945. First Performance: 26 November 1946, Prague, Czechoslovakia, Antonin Hyksa, viola, Jiří Berkovec, piano. First Publication: American Music Publisher, Inc., 2012.

Born in Prague, Karel Husa studied composition and conducting at the Prague Conservatory. From 1946–51 he furthered his studies with Nadia Boulanger and Arthur Honegger in Paris. In 1948, Husa returned to Czechoslovakia but was soon forced into exile as the new Communist regime in Prague banned him and his music. This ban would remain in effect until the fall of the Soviet Union in 1989. He moved to the United States in 1954 to take a position at Cornell University as Kappa Alpha Professor of Music. There he taught composition, conducting, and orchestration until his retirement in 1992. Husa has received numerous awards for his music, including the Lili Boulanger Prize, a Guggenheim Fellowship, and the Pulitzer Prize.

Husa's Suite for viola and piano is one of his earliest works. He composed it while he was still a student in Prague studying with neo-classical composer Jaroslav Řídký. Husa composed neo-classicism works as well, but the suite for viola and piano shows that Husa was already departing from this path, while not yet giving over entirely to the serialism with which he experimented in the late 1950s and early 1960s.

Bohuslav Martinů (1890–1959)
POCO ANDANTE
first movement from Sonata No. 1 for Viola and Piano

Date of Composition: 1955. Dedication: "To Lillian Fuchs." First Performance: 12 March 1956, New York City, Lillian Fuchs, viola, Artur Balsam, piano. First Publication: Associated Music Publishers, Inc., 1958.

Bohuslav Martinů was born in Polička, in what is now the Czech Republic. He entered the Prague Conservatory as a violin student in 1906, but having no interest in following the academic curriculum, he was expelled in June 1910. Martinů travelled to Italy, France, and Switzerland as a member of the Czech Philharmonic Orchestra, and from 1923–1940 he studied composition with Albert Roussel in Paris. He fled the Nazis and arrived in New York with his wife in 1941. While in the U.S., Martinů received important commissions, including one from Serge Koussevitzky for his First Symphony. Martinů lived and traveled widely in the United States and Europe, but never returned to his native Czechoslovakia.

Martinů's Sonata No. 1 for Viola and Piano is his sole viola sonata. An accomplished violinist and former member of the Czech Philharmonic, Martinů had a deep affinity for string instruments and wrote numerous chamber works for strings. This lyrical piece was inspired by violist Lillian Fuchs, whom he met in New York in 1947. Martinů composed the sonata between 22 November and 16 December 1955 during a period in his life when he struggled with depression and homesickness after returning to the United States to teach at the Curtis Institute following two years in Nice, France.

Bright Sheng (b. 1955)
THE STREAM FLOWS

Date of Composition: 1988. Dedication: "To Marlow Fisher." First Performance: 1991, Chicago, Li Kuo Chang, viola. First Publication: G. Schirmer, Inc., 1990.

Composer, conductor, and pianist Bright Sheng was born in Shanghai. During China's Cultural Revolution he was sent to the remote Qinghai province, which borders Tibet. When China's universities reopened in 1978, Sheng studied composition at the Shanghai Conservatory of Music. In 1982, he moved to New York City, where he studied with George Perle, Hugo Weisgall, Chou Wen-Chung, Jack Beeson, and Mario Davidovsky. In 1985, as a student at Tanglewood Music Center, Sheng met his future mentor Leonard Bernstein. Sheng studied composition and conducting privately with Bernstein until his passing in 1990. Sheng's compositions have won him many honors and awards, including three fellowships from the National Endowment for the Arts, a Charles Ives Scholarship Award from the American Academy and Institute of Arts and Letters, and fellowships and awards from the Guggenheim, Jerome, Naumberg, and Rockefeller Foundations. Sheng received the MacArthur Foundation Fellowship and the American Award in Music from the American Academy of Arts and Letters in 2001, and an ASCAP Achievement Award the following year.

Composer's note from the original publication:

The Stream Flows is based on a well-known Chinese folk song from the southern part of China. The freshness and richness of the tune deeply touched me when I first heard it. Since then, I have used it as basic material in several of my works. In this setting, the sound of the viola should evoke the timbre, and tone quality, of a female folk sing.

—Bright Sheng

THE STREAM FLOWS

The rising moon shines brightly,
It reminds me of my love in the mountains.

Like the moon, you walk in the sky,
As the crystal stream flows down the mountain.

A clear breeze blows up the hill.
My love, do you hear I am calling you?

Dmitri Shostakovich (1906–1975)
ADAGIO
third movement from Sonata for Viola and Piano, Op. 147

Date of Composition: 1975. Dedication: "To Fjodor Drushinin." First Performance: 1 October 1975, Glinka Hall, Leningrad, Soviet Union, Fyodor Druzhinin, viola, Mikhail Muntyan, piano. First Publication: G. Schirmer, Inc., 1975.

Shostakovich is a major mid-twentieth century composer, famous for his epic symphonies, concertos, string quartets, and other chamber works. Born in St. Petersburg, his entire career took place in Soviet-era Russia. Shostakovich composed the Sonata for Viola and Piano, Op. 147 between 1 July and 6 August 1975. It is the last piece he ever wrote, as he died three days later, on 9 August 1975, at a hospital in Kuntsevo. According to Fjodor Druzhinin, the violist to whom the work is dedicated and a member of the Beethoven Quartet which premiered thirteen of Shostakovich's fifteen string quartets, Shostakovich referred to the first movement as a novella, the second as a scherzo, and the finale as an adagio in memory of Beethoven. The final movement departs from a conventional fast tempo finale and draws extensive inspiration from Beethoven's "Moonlight" Sonata. Like many of his later works, such as the Thirteenth Quartet and the Fourteenth Symphony with eleven settings on the subject of death, the mood and theme of the sonata reflect Shostakovich's preoccupation with mortality.

Augusta Read Thomas (b. 1964)
CHANT
Date of Composition: 1989 (cello), 1991 (viola transcription), revised 2002. Dedication: "For Jeanne and Norman Fischer." First Performance: 21 January 1992, Rice University, Houston, Texas. First Performance of 2002 Revision: 16 April 2002, Merkin Concert Hall, New York City, Kate Dillingham, cello, Blair McMillen, piano. First Publication: G. Schirmer, Inc., 2005.

Augusta Read Thomas was born in Glen Cove, New York and studied composition with Oliver Knussen at Tanglewood, Jacob Druckman at Yale University, and Alan Stout and M. William Karlins at Northwestern University. Thomas is a member of the American Academy of Arts and Letters and she has won awards from the Tanglewood Music Center, the Aspen Music Festival, ASCAP, BMI, the National Endowment for the Arts, the American Academy and Institute of Arts and Letters, and the Guggenheim, Koussevitzky, Naumburg, Rockefeller, and Fromm Foundations. Thomas has been on faculty at the Eastman School of Music and Northwestern University. She currently serves on the Dean's Music Advisory Board at Northwestern University, and often teaches at the Tanglewood Music Center.

Program note from the original publication:

Augusta Read Thomas' *Chant* for violoncello and piano (now withdrawn) was composed in 1989. A new version, commissioned by cellist Kate Dillingham, was created in 2002. This edition for viola and piano, based on the 2002 version, has been transcribed by the composer. The full work lasts 11 minutes. The composer provides an option of ending the work after 9½ minutes. The pianist should observe all pedal indications but may otherwise pedal freely. All grace notes are to be played before the beat.

Notes by Rachel Kelly

Dedicated to Milton Preves

Meditation and Processional
I. Meditation

Ernest Bloch

34

38

42

46

II. Processional

il basso pronunziato

Processional

second movement from *Suite hebraïque* for Viola and Piano

Ernest Bloch

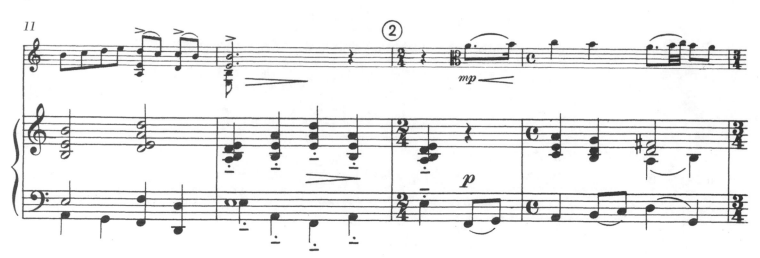

Lento
third movement from Suite for Viola and Piano

Ernest Bloch

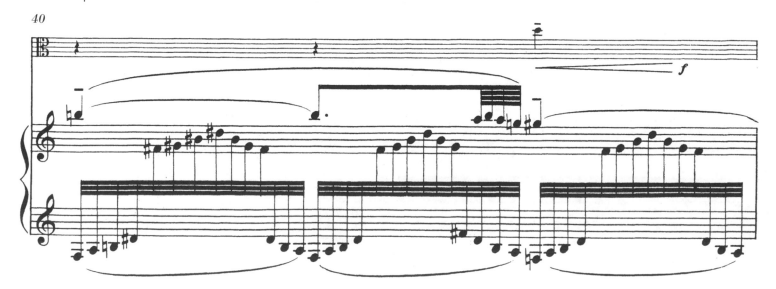

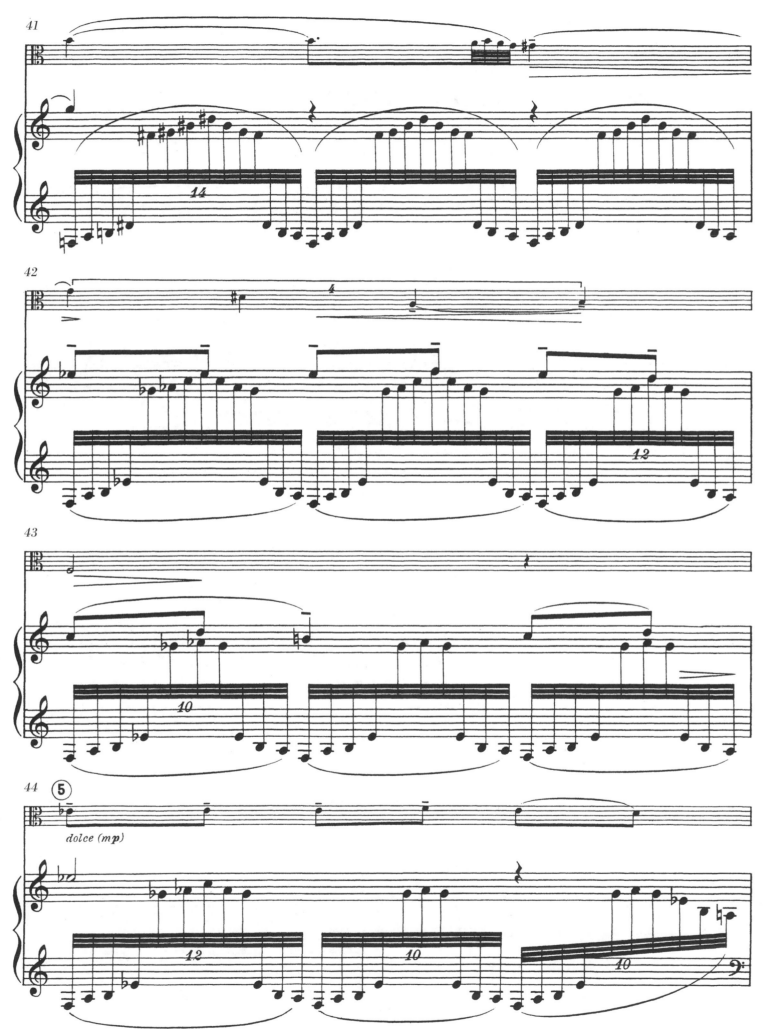

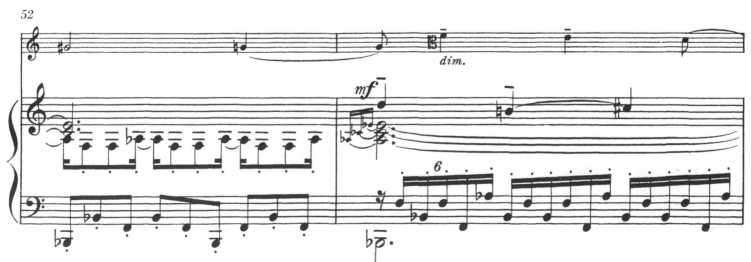

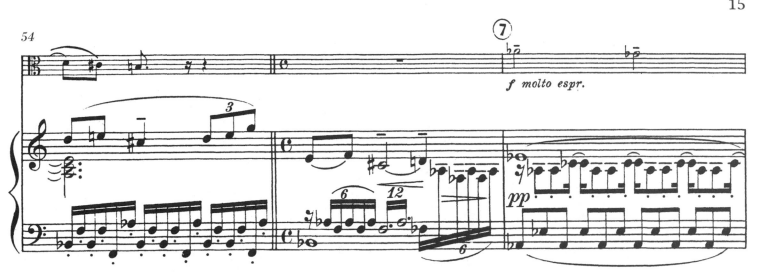

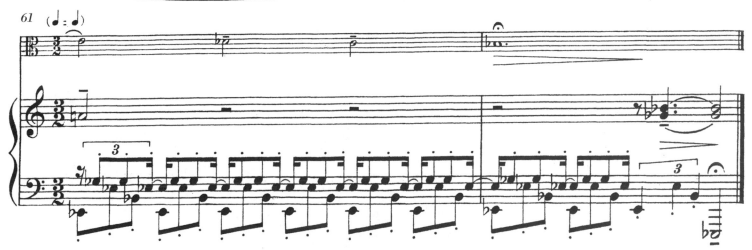

To BB

Passacaglia
on an Old English Tune*

Rebecca Clarke

* Attributed to Thomas Tallis

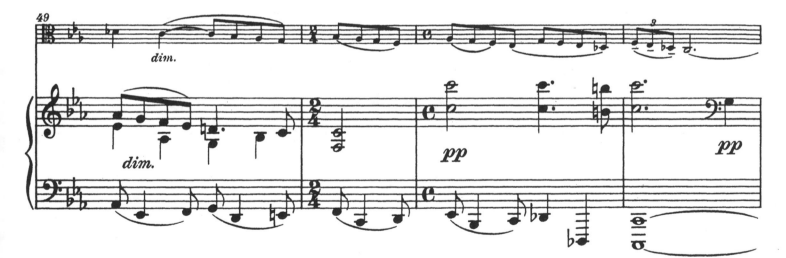

Elegie
second movement from Suite for Viola and Piano, Op. 5

Karel Husa

un poco più mosso

To Lillian Fuchs

Poco Andante
first movement from Sonata No. 1 for Viola and Piano

Viola part edited
by Lillian Fuchs

Bohuslav Martinů

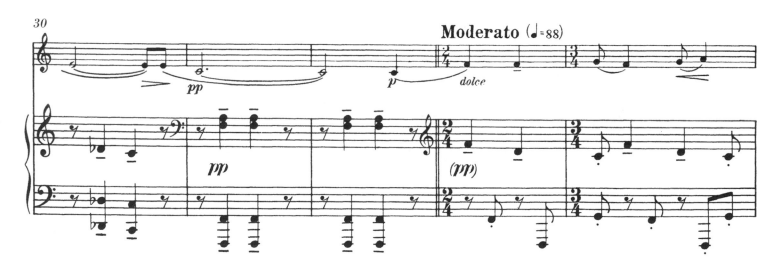

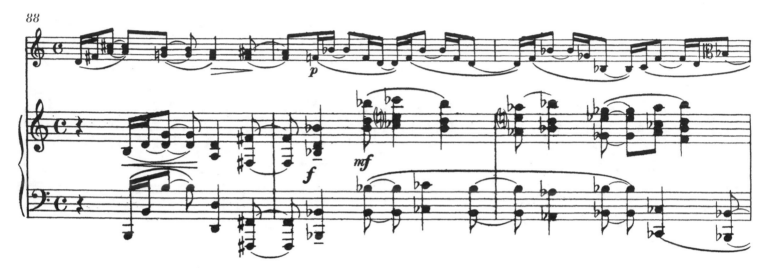

THE
G.SCHIRMER
VIOLA ANTHOLOGY
11 WORKS FROM THE 20TH AND 21ST CENTURIES

See Viola/Piano Score for
Notes on the Music

ISBN 978-1-4803-9526-8

ED 4572

G. SCHIRMER, *Inc.*

DISTRIBUTED BY

HAL•LEONARD®
CORPORATION
7777 W. BLUEMOUND RD. P.O. BOX 13819 MILWAUKEE, WI 53213

www.musicsalesclassical.com
www.halleonard.com

CONTENTS

WORKS FOR VIOLA AND PIANO

WORKS FOR SOLO VIOLA

Dedicated to Milton Preves

Meditation and Processional
I. Meditation

Ernest Bloch

II. Processional

Processional

second movement from *Suite hebraïque* for Viola and Piano

Ernest Bloch

Lento

third movement from Suite for Viola and Piano

Ernest Bloch

To BB

Passacaglia
on an Old English Tune*

Rebecca Clarke

Grave, ma non troppo lento

---

* Attributed to Thomas Tallis

Fancy on a Bach Air
for solo viola

Edited by
Melia Watras

John Corigliano

The Violist's Notebook

Book One

I.

(Marcus Thompson)

John Harbison

II.
(Betty Hauck)

III.

(James Dunham)

14

IV.
(Kim Kashkashian)

Appassionato ♩. = 60–69

V.
(Mary Ruth Ray)

Rubato, improvisando

♩. = 80

VI.
(Marcus Thompson)

Elegie
second movement from Suite for Viola and Piano, Op. 5

Karel Husa

To Lillian Fuchs

Poco Andante
first movement from Sonata No. 1 for Viola and Piano

Viola part edited by Lillian Fuchs

Bohuslav Martinů

Tempo I

Adagio
third movement from Sonata for Viola and Piano, Op. 147

Dmitri Shostakovich

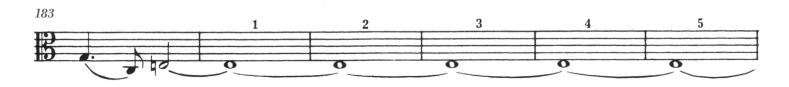

for Jeanne and Norman Fischer

Chant
for Viola and Piano

Augusta Read Thomas

N.B.: Grace notes come before the beat.

*The use of a mute for bars 72 through 98 is optional.

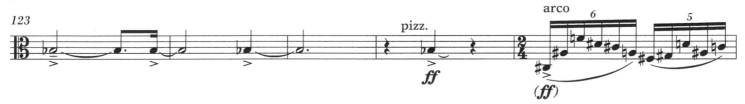

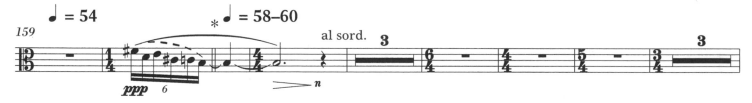

*The piece may, optionally, end here.

to Marlow Fisher

The Stream Flows

Bright Sheng

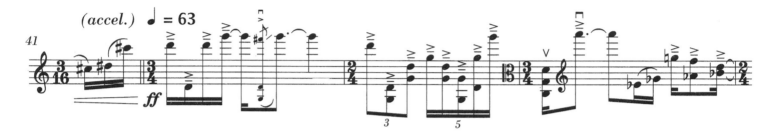

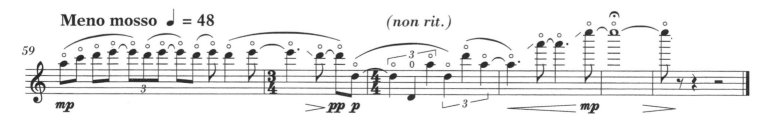

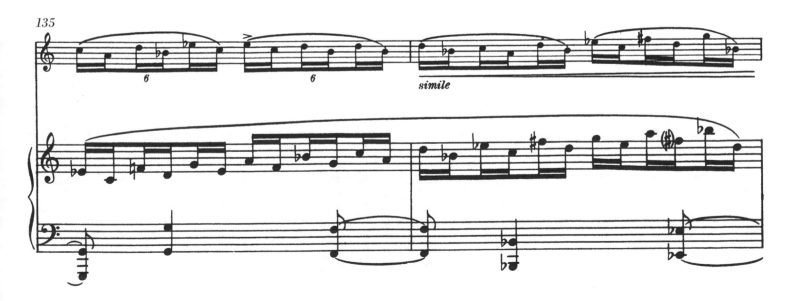

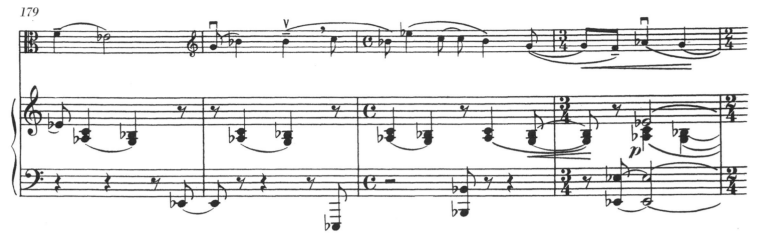

for Jeanne and Norman Fischer

Chant
for Viola and Piano

Augusta Read Thomas

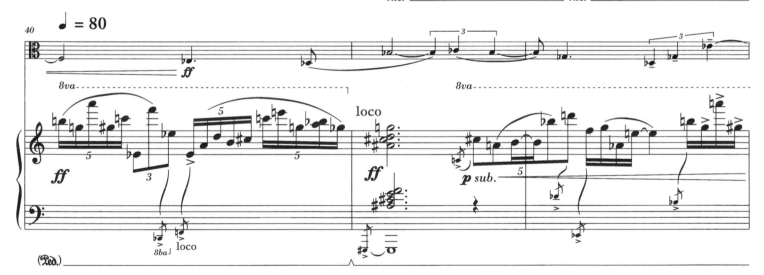

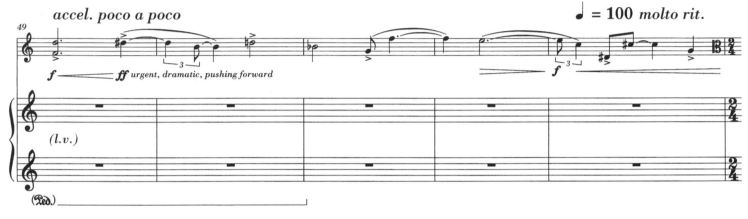

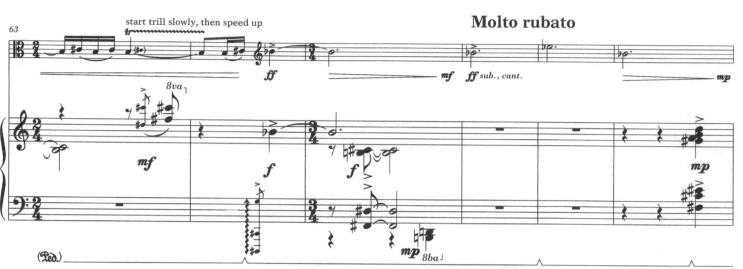

*The use of a mute for bars 72 through 98 is optional.

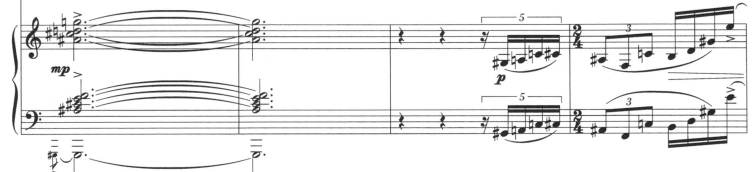

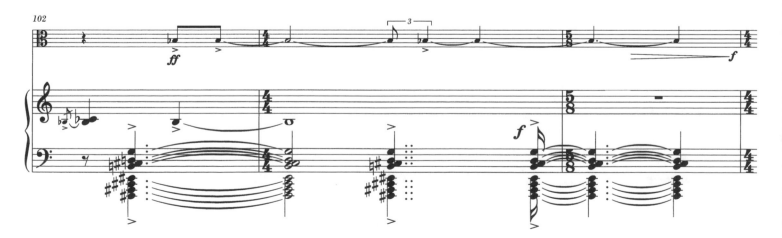

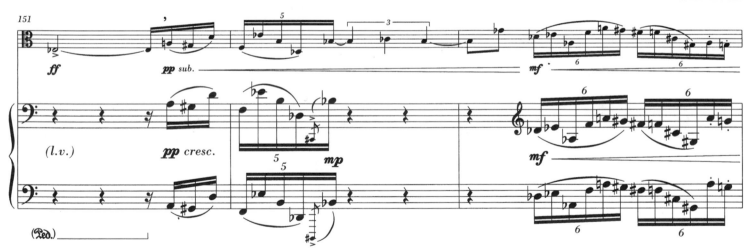

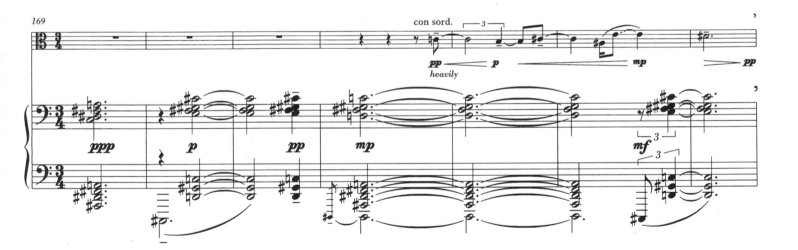

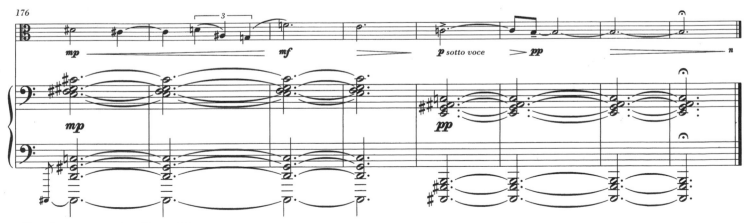

*The piece may, optionally, end here.

Adagio
third movement from Sonata for Viola and Piano, Op. 147

Dmitri Shostakovich

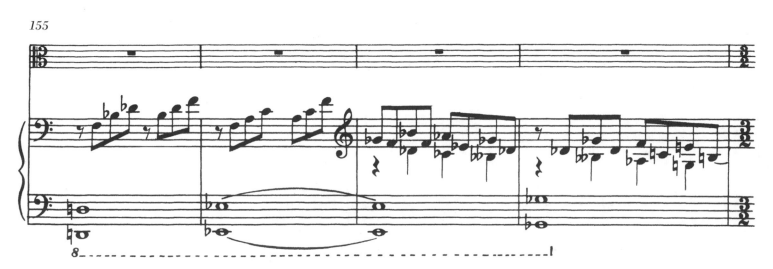

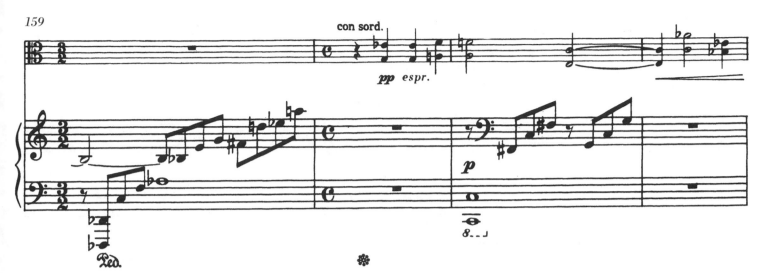